QUICK START DRAMA FOR WORSHIP

Readers Theatre

LILLENAS
DRAMA

QUICK START DRAMA FOR WORSHIP

Readers Theatre

Lillenas PUBLISHING COMPANY
KANSAS CITY, MO 64141

Copyright © 2005 by Lillenas Publishing Company

All print rights administered by Lillenas Publishing Co. All rights reserved.

Printed in the United States.

Scripture quotations are from the *Holy Bible, New International Version*® (NIV®). Copyright © 1973, 1978, 1984 by International Bible Society. Used by permission of Zondervan Publishing House. All rights reserved.

The purchase of this book entitles the purchaser to make photocopies of this material for use in their church or nonprofit organization. Sharing of the material in this book with other churches or organizations not owned or controlled by the original purchaser is prohibited. The contents of this book may not be reproduced in any other form without written permission from the publisher. Please include the above copyright statement on each copy made. These scripts are protected by copyright. No changes may be made to these scripts in any form without written permission from the publisher.

Questions? Please write or call:
   Lillenas Publishing Company
   Drama Resources
   P.O. Box 419527
   Kansas City, MO 64141
   Phone: 816-931-1900 • Fax: 816-412-8390
   E-mail: drama@lillenas.com
   Web site: www.lillenasdrama.com

Cover art by Darlene Filley

Contents

Friends of Job	7
Theme: God is in control	
The Gift	10
Theme: Salvation	
Face of Jesus	13
Theme: When hatred and envy take a hold of our hearts, it's hard to see the face of Jesus.	
In Spirit and in Truth	16
Themes: Christian Living, worship	
Psalm 23	21
Theme: Trusting God, renewal, God's peace	
Sssin and Sssuffering	25
Themes: Deception, consequences of sin, the sinful nature	
Christ's Body	28
Themes: The Body of Christ, spiritual gifts, community	
Jesus Heals a Man Born Blind	32
Theme: The healing power of Jesus	
Condemned	36
Themes: Maundy Thursday, Good Friday, Easter	
Love's Gift	39
Themes: Christmas, giving	

Friends of Job

by Jeff Smith & Wayne Sigler

Running Time: 3 minutes

Theme: God is in control

Scripture References: Job 38:2; 1 Corinthians 13:12

Synopsis: When Lisa's husband left her, she left God. In her search for hope, her "friends" try to persuade her to listen to each of their opinions.

Cast:
   Lisa—Age 30-35
   Friend 1—Age 30-35
   Friend 2—Age 30-35
   Friend 3—Age 30-35
   Blake—Lisa's teenage son, age 13-17

Production Notes: Lisa sits CS on a stool or a chair. Friends 1, 2, 3, and Blake stand US of her in a semicircle, SR to SL respectively, with their backs to the audience.

Lisa: I didn't see it coming. Others did . . . but not me. Just because the car knocks doesn't mean that it's ready to be junked, right? I thought Frank and I just needed a tune-up after 15 years. My friends tell me I can be pretty naive.

Friend 1 *(turning in place to face* Lisa*)*: He's using you, Lisa. He just wants you to keep the home fires burning until he gets back from the hunt.

Friend 2 *(turning in place to face* Lisa*)*: The Word doesn't promise us we won't be without problems. James 1:2-3 says, "Consider it pure joy, my brothers, whenever you face trials of many kinds, because you know that the testing of your faith develops perseverance."

Friend 1: You're better off without him. Men! Who needs them?

Friend 2: You have made a solemn vow before God and other witnesses; a covenant, Lisa. By being divorced from him you could cause someone else to stumble and commit adultery. Matthew 5:32 says, "Anyone who marries the divorced woman commits adultery."

Friend 3 *(turning in place to face* Lisa*)*: There are two sides to every story. Frank was obviously unhappy in this relationship. Why?

"Friends of Job" is taken from *Free Floating*. Copyright © 1998 by Jeff Smith and Wayne Sigler. All print rights administered by Lillenas® Publishing Co. All rights reserved. Printed in the United States.

(FRIENDS 1, 2, 3 *return to their original positions.*)

LISA: Everybody had a different opinion on what was right and wrong. The only thing I knew was how I felt: I was angry, hurt, and still in love with Frank. I desperately wanted him back.

BLAKE (*turning in place to face* LISA): You've got to be kidding, Mom! After what he's done to you . . . to us! He doesn't love us. You're crazy for wanting him back. I hope he never comes back. Never!

(BLAKE *returns to original position.*)

LISA: I just wanted to stay in bed, pull up the covers, and die. Actually, the pain is the only thing that made me remember that I was still alive.

(FRIENDS 1, 2, 3, *and* BLAKE *turn and face* LISA.)

FRIEND 1/BLAKE: Curse him.

FRIEND 2: You'll be cursed.

FRIEND 3: It's a curse to get older.

(FRIENDS 1, 2, 3, *and* BLAKE *return to their original places.*)

LISA: God was nowhere. I prayed and heard nothing. I went to church and was miserable. It's funny, but when Frank left me, I left God. But He waited . . . just like I waited for Frank; faithful, devoted, committed . . . all the things I hated myself for being. Finally, I got back in the Bible and His words . . . words without condemnation . . . wooed me back.

(LISA *picks up a Bible positioned near the stool and opens it. The players behind her provide the voice to the words.*)

FRIEND 1 (*moves toward* LISA *and puts a hand on her shoulder*): "Be still, and know that I am God; I will be exalted among the nations, I will be exalted in the earth." (Psalm 46:10)

FRIEND 2 (*moves toward* LISA): "Be strong and courageous. Do not be afraid or terrified because of them, for the Lord your God goes with you; he will never leave you nor forsake you." (Deuteronomy 31:6)

FRIEND 3 (*moves toward* LISA): "He who dwells in the shelter of the Most High will rest in the shadow of the Almighty." (Psalm 91:1)

BLAKE (*moves toward* LISA *and puts a hand on her shoulder*): "Trust in the Lord with all your heart and lean not on your own understanding; in all your ways acknowledge him, and he will make your paths straight." (Proverbs 3:5)

LISA: No answers as to why; no explanations; just hope. Something no one else could give me. It's funny, but when everyone abandoned me and I left God, He stayed. He took me back like I took Frank back eventually. It's not all happily-ever-after. I lost a lot; friends *(FRIENDS 1, 2, 3 return to their original positions)*, trust *(BLAKE returns to his original position)*, and confidence. But God gave me back something immeasurably more important . . . HOPE.

The Gift

by Courtney Walsh

Running Time: Approximately 7-8 minutes

Theme: Salvation

Scripture Reference: John 3:16

Synopsis: This piece is a bit different from the typical sketch. It is a narration about the love God has for us as children. It takes the audience through a series of emotions, many of which are common among those who are contemplating salvation. As the reading begins, two actors, one playing God and one playing the Sinner, can be seen on the stage. They act out the words as the Narrator continues, but have no lines. Their expressions and blocking change according to the narration. This is a good way to see into the mind of the Sinner, to show that none of us are alone in the thoughts that we are unworthy of God's precious gift: the gift of eternal life.

Cast:
NARRATOR—Can be male or female; should have a good speaking voice
GOD
SINNER—Male or female

Production Notes:
Actors—It is important not to be overly dramatic. While it will be difficult to act without using any words, there still must be an element of realism. Having the God character onstage is optional.
Props—The Gift—a big white box beautifully (professionally) wrapped, situated just out of the lit area of the stage.
Costumes—At the direction of the director
Set—None needed
Sound—While it's not essential, you may want to consider adding sound effects such as a beating heart or the sound of breathing where they are mentioned in the script.
Lights—It is effective to have a large, bright light at the back of the stage pointing toward the audience for the moment when God enters.

(Lights up slowly. SINNER *is seen, confused, as if in a fog.* NARRATOR *is SR.)*

NARRATOR: You think perhaps you are dreaming. You feel like you are moving in slow motion or swimming through water. You can hear the sound of your breathing. It echoes in your head. You walk along until you are stopped by a great white light. *(Light from backstage turns on, startling the*

Copyright © 2004 by Courtney Walsh. All print rights administered by Lillenas® Publishing Co. All rights reserved. Printed in the United States.

audience.) In front of you, you are sure, is God. His face emerges from the brightness. *(*GOD *enters.)* It is gentle and pure. It is perfect, like nothing you've ever seen.

In His eyes you can see compassion. It is unmistakable. You can't imagine what He must be thinking as He looks at you—this little person with a whole sea of problems. Still, in His presence you feel this tremendous peace. And you think for the first time in a long time that everything is going to be OK.

Then God does something you don't expect. He turns from you and picks something up. As He turns back, you see it is a gift. It's a big gift, beautifully wrapped with the most exceptional bows and paper you've ever seen. It is spotless. As He looks at you, you see the joy in His eyes, the smile on His face. He is proud of this gift, and it is clear He cannot wait for you to open the package and see what's inside.

You smile back, politely. You stretch your hands out to God. You want to take the gift, but then you remember who you are. You're not the person He meant to give it to. You're the sinner. You're the one who has a list of regrets, too many to remember. Doesn't He know you aren't worthy of this gift?

The expression on the face of God changes. You notice. He looks hurt somehow. As though you've rejected Him. Or maybe He simply wonders why you're not jumping to get the gift, why you would hesitate. He wants to say something to you, but He is a gentleman. He doesn't want to overstep His bounds. You look up, into the face of God, and wonder why on earth He would offer you a gift. You've offered Him nothing. Not one thing up until this point have you given. Oh, He's asked. He's asked for your heart, but you selfishly refused to give it. You wanted to keep it for yourself.

Now you can hear that heart pounding. It's a decision you have to make. How can you turn and walk away? His face is so intent. He wants badly to give you this present. He spent so much time picking it out and making it perfect. He took it home, wrapped it up and made it look as perfect on the outside as it really was on the inside. You look away from the intense gaze of the Father. You start to turn. In the corner of your eye you see the expression on His face. The pained look is so harrowing that you immediately begin to weep. God begins to turn away. He is, as always, a gentleman and does not want to force you to take what He is offering. The choice, He has made clear, is up to you. Your heartbeat quickens. You feel the pounding on the inside of your chest. God has paused, hoping you will change your mind. You think of what this means. You wonder what will change. How will this shape your life? Will you still be the same person and what if you can't live up to God's expectations? What if you fail? What if you disgrace His name and do the very things you're now so sorry you've done?

And then it's as though He is reading your mind. His hand reaches out and touches your face. He looks down at you with a knowing look and says,

"I'll love you anyway, my child."

One single tear begins to trickle down your cheek. It is met by the finger of the Lord, your face wiped clean, just like your blemishes on your slate.

"Just like I love you now."

You know this is not a gift you deserve. You think perhaps it's not a gift you want, but deep down, you are certain it is a gift you need. For somehow, somewhere, deep in the pit of your soul, there is an emptiness. There is a hole that only this gift can fill.

Quietly, you look at God one more time, convinced that He will change His mind when you tell Him all the things you have thought or done. But as you begin to speak, He quiets you, gently.

"Be still and know that I am God," He says.

"Your past is in the past. I know in your heart you are sorry. And I forgive you. Take the gift I am offering and you will have eternal life."

You are quiet. Your heart is heavy. You cannot believe the grace that God has shown you. You don't deserve to be forgiven; yet He forgave you. You don't deserve to be loved, yet He loves you. You don't deserve to be His child, yet He calls you His son, His daughter. Carefully, you reach up and take the gift He is holding. Jesus. Savior. The perfect Lamb of God. The only One who will save us all from our sins. And all you have to do is believe in Him and accept Him. The gift is yours.

Face of Jesus

by Dave Tippett

Running Time: Approximately 4 minutes

Theme: When hatred and envy take a hold of our hearts, it's hard to see the face of Jesus.

Synopsis: A story told of Leonardo da Vinci, his "The Last Supper," and a rival painter.

Cast: Teens or adults, either gender for all readers
  Reader 1
  Reader 2
  Reader 3
  Reader 4

Production Notes: There is an empty set. The readers will face forward while there is a PowerPoint slide of "The Last Supper" painting behind them.

Reader 1: At the time that Leonardo da Vinci painted "The Last Supper,"

Reader 2: he had an enemy who was a fellow painter.

Reader 3: An enemy.

Reader 4: An enemy.

Reader 1: da Vinci had had a bitter argument with this man.

Reader 2: da Vinci despised the man.

Reader 3: An enemy.

Reader 4: Bitter argument.

Reader 1: When da Vinci painted the face of Judas Iscariot at the table with Jesus

Reader 2: —for his masterwork "The Last Supper"—

Reader 3: he used the face of his enemy so that

Reader 4: it would be present for ages as the man

Reader 2: who betrayed Jesus.

Reader 3: His enemy.

Copyright © 2002 by Dave Tippett. All print rights administered by Lillenas® Publishing Co. All rights reserved. Printed in the United States.

READER 4: da Vinci took delight while painting this picture—

READER 2: in knowing that others would actually

READER 3: notice the face of His enemy on Judas.

READER 4: His enemy.

READER 1: As da Vinci worked on the faces of the other disciples,

READER 2: he often tried to paint the face of Jesus—

READER 3: but could not make any progress.

READER 4: Painting the face of Jesus,

READER 1: da Vinci felt

READER 2: frustrated.

READER 3: Confused.

READER 4: Painting the face of Jesus.

READER 1: In time he realized

READER 2: what was wrong.

READER 3: His hatred—

READER 4: for the other painter—

READER 2: his enemy—

READER 3: was holding him back—

READER 4: from finishing the face

READER 2: of Jesus.

READER 3: The face of Jesus.

READER 4: The face of Jesus.

READER 1: Only after making peace with his fellow painter—

READER 2: his enemy no more—

READER 3: and repainting the face of Judas,

READER 4: was da Vinci able to paint the face of Jesus—

READER 2: the face of Jesus—

READER 3: and complete his masterpiece.

READER 4: Today, many enemies

Reader 1: leave us

Reader 2: frustrated.

Reader 3: Confused.

Reader 4: Keeping us from

Reader 1: the face of Jesus.

Reader 3: Hatred holds us back

Reader 4: from the face of Jesus.

Reader 2: But the face of Jesus

Reader 1: frees us

Reader 3: to complete

Reader 4: a true masterpiece, which is

Reader 1: peace with an enemy.

Reader 2: Peace.

Reader 3: A masterpiece—

Reader 4: Indeed.

(Blackout)

In Spirit and in Truth

by Kevin Stoltz

Running Time: Approximately 5-7 minutes

Theme: Worship, Christian living

Scripture References: Psalm 96:1, 11-12; John 4:22-24

Synopsis: A readers theatre script on the essence of worship and the perspective it gives to the Christian life.

Cast:
  Reader 1
  Reader 2
  Reader 3
  Reader 4
  Reader 5

Production Notes: A readers theatre for five people; may be any combination of men and women. The script can stand on its own or could follow a medley of songs, with the hymn "All Hail the Power of Jesus' Name."

The readers stand on the stage with Reader 1 at SR, and then in numerical order the other readers stand to his left, forming a straight line.

In certain places of the script there are lines with no punctuation, these lines are to be read as one continuous sentence so that the flow of speech is uninterrupted.

Reader 1 *(triumphant):* All hail the power of Jesus' name!

All *(triumphant, said the same as* Reader 1*):* All hail the power of Jesus' name!

Reader 2 *(a little less excited):* All hail the power.

Reader 3 *(matter-of-fact):* All hail.

Reader 4: A bit traditional.

Reader 1: It is worshipful.

Reader 5: But it should do.

Reader 2: What is a diadem? *(All other* Readers *turn and look at* Reader 2; *slight pause.)*

"In Spirit and in Truth" is taken from *The Lamb and the Wolf*. Copyright © 1998 by Kevin Stoltz. All print rights administered by Lillenas® Publishing Co. All rights reserved. Printed in the United States.

READER 4: Traditional is archaic.

READER 3: It is safe.

READER 4: Is it too familiar?

(For the next four lines use a singsong pattern.)

READER 2: I will enter His gates

READERS 2, 5: with thanksgiving in . . .

(READERS 1 *and* 3 *look at others in dismay.*)

READERS 2, 4, 5: my heart.

READERS 2, 4, 5: I will enter . . .

READER 1: Contemporary is repetitive,

READER 3: theologically shallow.

READER 5: It is worshipful.

READER 2: I will enter His courts with

READER 4: Praise!

ALL: Praise!

(Next few lines pick up speed and tempo.)

READER 2: Saxophone

READER 1: Organ

READER 3: Drums

READER 5: Piano

READER 4: Synthesizer

READER 1: Strings

READER 3: Bass

READER 4: Woodwinds

READER 5: Percussion

READER 1 *(joyous):* Sing to the Lord

READER 2: a new song,

READER 3: all the earth.

READER 4 *(puzzled):* New?

READER 5: And bless His name!

READER 4 *(puzzled):* Specifically, what is new?

(Pause. Other READERS look at READER 4 questioningly, then at each other, and then answer somewhat hesitantly.)

READER 1: Sing

READER 2: to the

READER 3: Lord

READER 1, 2, 3, 5: a new

READER 1: song.

(Pause. READERS 1, 2, 3, 5 look at each other, then at READER 4.)

READERS 1, 2, 3, 5 *(said the same as READER 4):* Specifically, what is new?

READER 4: It is not old,

READER 1: or traditional,

READER 2: or contemporary.

READER 3 *(steps forward then freezes):* It goes beyond hymn singing,

READER 1 *(takes step forward and freezes):* beyond choruses,

READER 5 *(takes step forward and freezes):* beyond drama,

READER 2 *(takes step forward and freezes):* beyond liturgy,

READER 4 *(takes step forward and freezes):* beyond . . . ?

(Pause)

READER 1: That is our dilemma.

(Other READERS unfreeze.)

READER 2: We

READER 5: are told

READER 3: to sing

ALL: a new song.

READER 4: What is new . . . is beyond ourselves?

READER 2: What?

READER 4: That which is new is beyond me.

READER 5: It is beyond me?

READER 3: It is beyond us,

READER 2: our actions,

READER 1: our performance,

READER 3: our planning.

READER 4: A new song

READER 1: is the Spirit.

READER 5: They that worship Him,

READER 4: worship Him

READER 2: in Spirit

READER 5: and in truth.

READER 3: A new song!

READER 5: Spirit!

READER 3: Truth!

ALL: Sing to the Lord a NEW SONG!

(Pause)

READER 1: Traditional—

READER 3: Let the heavens be glad!

READER 5: Dramatic—

READER 2: Woodwinds and strings,

READER 4: Hymns and choruses.

READER 3: Let the earth rejoice!

READER 1: Contemporary—

READER 2: Brass

READER 5: Liturgical—

READER 4: Synthesizer

READER 3: The fields rejoice!

READER 2: Percussion

READER 3: All the trees of the forest sing!

ALL: Come, let us worship.

(Pause)

READER 5: Serve the Lord with gladness, come before Him with joyful singing. *(Turns around)*

READER 4: Know that the Lord himself is God. *(Turns around)*

READER 3: We are His people, and the sheep of His pasture. *(Turns around)*

READER 2: Give thanks to Him, and bless His name. *(Turns around)*

Reader 1: His loving-kindness is everlasting, and His faithfulness to all generations. *(Turns around)*

(Slight pause, then the READERS *exit to either SL or SR.)*

Psalm 23

by Chuck Neighbors

Running Time: 6 minutes

Themes: Trusting God, renewal, God's peace

Scripture Reference: Psalm 23

Synopsis: A voice of conscience and two voices of truth explain Psalm 23 and what it means to have the Lord as your shepherd.

Cast:
  READER 1—Truth speaker
  READER 2—Truth speaker
  READER 3—A seeker characterized by confusion and questions
  READER 4—A questioner; a voice of conscience

Props:
  Scripts in a black binder to strike a uniform appearance

Production Note: There is no particular setting. Cast may stand or sit on stools (or a combination of both). Readers 1 and 2 on the outside and Readers 3 and 4 on the inside. As with all readers theatre, it is good to stage the cast in a creative manner; use different levels if possible, and avoid lining up the cast in a straight line.

READER 1: The Lord is my Shepherd,

READER 2: I shall not be in want.

READER 3: I don't know. I mean, I believe in God and Jesus and all that stuff. But I still *want*. There are lots and lots of things I would just love to have.

READER 4: But are you *in* want? Have you learned the secret that the apostle Paul learned? He says:

READER 1: "I have learned the secret of being content in any and every situation, whether well fed or hungry, whether living in plenty or in want. I can do everything through him who gives me strength."

READER 3: Hey, I'm no Paul . . . but, I guess, when you put it that way . . .

READER 4: Is the Lord your Shepherd?

"Psalm 23" is taken from *The "What Would Jesus Do?" Playbook*. Copyright © 1999 by Chuck Neighbors. All print rights administered by Lillenas® Publishing Co. All rights reserved. Printed in the United States.

READER 2: He makes me lie down in green pastures.

READER 3: Not me, man! You gotta be kidding. I'm not gonna lie down in any pastures. You know what hangs out in pastures, don't you? I mean, you don't know what else has been there—if you get my drift. I have a hard enough time not stepping in it—I sure ain't gonna lie in it.

READER 1: He leads me beside still waters.

READER 3: Yeah, well, lately the water is a little too still. The word "stagnant" comes to mind.

READER 1: He restores my soul.

READER 3: If only that were true.

READER 4: If you don't appreciate the green pastures, if the water is stagnant—then you need to be restored. To be restored implies that you have spent yourself in service to God. To restore means to refresh, to revive, to bring you back to the way you were before you spent yourself—serving Him. Peter says this?

READER 2: "And the God of all grace, who called you to his eternal glory in Christ, after you have suffered a little while, will himself restore you and make you strong, firm and steadfast."

READER 3: OK. OK. I get your point. But, man, it's a crazy world out there. How do I "spend" myself when I have so many other pressures weighing me down? I need restoring, but I'm not exactly knocking myself out for Jesus. Life's pretty complicated, ya know? What's He expect, anyway?

READER 4: Is the Lord your Shepherd?

READER 1: He guides me in paths of righteousness for His name's sake.

READER 3: Hey, OK, I know, righteousness. That's what He expects. Hey, I try to do the right thing—but I'm only human, ya know? It ain't easy.

READER 4: No one said that it would be. But Paul said . . .

READER 3: Not him again.

READER 4: Paul said:

READER 1: "Those who live according to the sinful nature have their minds set on what that nature desires; but those who live in accordance with the Spirit have their minds set on what the Spirit desires. The mind of sinful man is death, but the mind controlled by the Spirit is life and peace."

READER 3: Hey, are you trying to scare me? I sin—I admit that. But I also believe. I want life, man—not death!

READER 4: Is the Lord your Shepherd?

READER 2: Even though I walk through the valley of the shadow of death . . .

READER 3: Uh, that valley of death thing. That's one walk I don't want to take.

READER 4: Are you afraid of shadows?

READER 3: Huh?

READER 4: It's not death—it's only shadow.

READER 3: Oh.

READER 1: I will fear no evil, for you are with me.

READER 3: That sounds good. But . . . I am afraid . . . some of the time . . . a little . . .

READER 4: His love drives out fear. Remember that God has said:

READER 2: "Never will I leave you. Never will I forsake you."

READER 3: Yeah. I'll try to remember that.

READER 4: Is the Lord your Shepherd?

READER 1: Your rod and your staff,

READER 2: they comfort me.

READER 3: Comfort? Half the time I feel like He would just as soon clobber me with them. Like when I do something wrong—here comes the rod! Wham!

READER 4: Then you don't understand shepherds.

READER 3: What do you mean?

READER 4: A shepherd's rod and staff was used to guide, rescue, and protect his sheep. In the Old Testament they were used as instruments to show God's support and power.

READER 3: I never thought of it that way before.

READER 4: Is the Lord your Shepherd?

READER 1: You prepare a table before me in the presence of my enemies.

READER 3: Wham! There it is again! Just when I begin to think nice warm fuzzies about God, I have enough trouble trying to get away from my enemies —now He invites them to dinner!

READER 4: It's His table—not theirs. Nobody said that they would be eating. To sit at the table with Him is to affirm His promises to you—His promise to be your Shepherd. Your enemies can't touch you while you're at His table.

READER 3: Oh. Well, that's comforting.

READER 4: That's the idea. Is the Lord your Shepherd?

READER 2: You anoint my head with oil.

READER 3: Yuck! I hate that look. Is that necessary?

READER 4: It's a sign of honor. You're the guest of honor.

READER 3: Really? Well, that's cool. *(Pause)* Why me?

READER 4: Why, indeed?

READER 3: Well?

READER 4: He loves you. Is the Lord your Shepherd?

READER 1: My cup overflows.

READER 3: I better drink up. What're we drinking?

READER 4: His blessings.

READER 3: Oh.

READER 4: Is the Lord your Shepherd?

READER 3: I . . . uh . . . want Him to be. How?

READER 4: Just ask Him.

READER 3: That simple?

READER 4: Yes. Then trust Him. Obey Him.

READER 3: That's the catch?

READER 4: That's the catch. Is the Lord your Shepherd?

READER 2: Surely goodness and love

READER 1: will follow me all the days of my life,

READERS 1, 2: and I will dwell in the house of the Lord forever.

READER 3 *(not sure):* Amen?

READERS 1, 2: Amen.

READER 4: Is the Lord your Shepherd?

The End

Sssin and Sssuffering

by Jeff Smith

Running Time: 3 minutes

Themes: Deception, consequences of sin, the sinful nature

Scripture References: Genesis 3; 1 Peter 5:8

Synopsis: A creative readers theatre piece about Eve's temptation.

Cast:
NARRATOR—Male or Female; nondescript
SERPENT—Male; deceptive, cunning, sly
EVE—Female; naive, innocent

Production Notes: Set in the Garden of Eden, this piece can be played as a readers theatre piece or can be acted out between the Serpent and Eve with the Narrator looking onto the action. Stage directions are indicated in the script.

NARRATOR: Silently.

SERPENT: Ssss

NARRATOR: Stalking, spying . . .

SERPENT: Ssss

NARRATOR: Slippery scoundrel stepping softly . . . shadows.

SERPENT: Ssss

NARRATOR: Serpent stops. Sees servant sleeping . . . sunset. Smiles.

SERPENT: Shhh

NARRATOR: Sneaky.

SERPENT: Surprise!

NARRATOR: Servant startled.

SERPENT: So . . .

NARRATOR: says the serpent,

SERPENT: Sodmaker says servant species shouldn't savor succulent seeds!

"Sssin and Sssuffering" is taken from *No Limits*. Copyright © 2003 by Jeff Smith. All print rights administered by Lillenas® Publishing Co. All rights reserved. Printed in the United States.

EVE: Silly!

NARRATOR: Servant says still somewhat sleepy.

EVE: Sodmaker says servant species should savor succulent seed as sustenance . . . 'cept in center.

SERPENT: Center? Ssss . . .

EVE: Sodmaker says savoring and sensing center succulent seed is sacred.

NARRATOR: Serpent snarls.

SERPENT: Sacred? *(Snarls)* Sodmaker's seed sacred? Senseless.

NARRATOR: Serpent simmers. Sun setting. Seconds slipping. Silence . . . Strategy.

SERPENT: Sliver? Slice? Sure sounds selfish.

NARRATOR: Servant shrugs.

SERPENT: Suppose . . .

NARRATOR: Servant squirms.

EVE: Suppose?

NARRATOR: Serpent circles servant.

SERPENT: Suppose Sodmaker's scared?

EVE: Sodmaker? Scared? Scandalous!

NARRATOR: Serpent circles servant.

SERPENT: Suppose Sodmaker's scared servants savor succulent seed in center and see.

EVE: See?

NARRATOR: Servant shudders. Serpent circles servant.

SERPENT: Yesss. Sees similar to Sodmaker.

NARRATOR: Serpent strikes. Servant swoons. Is she swayed?

EVE: Sees similar?

NARRATOR: She swallows.

SERPENT: Yesss. Sees shadows. Sees sunshine. Sees superior . . . smarter.

NARRATOR: She stalls. Seconds slipping. Soon Sabbath. Serpent stalks.

SERPENT: Someone should say something.

NARRATOR: Serpent circles.

SERPENT: Slavery should stop!

NARRATOR: Serpent circles.

SERPENT: Sodmaker's system seems strangely suspicious.

EVE: Yesss, suspicious.

NARRATOR: Serpent still circles.

SERPENT: Servant sees?

EVE: Yesss. Sees.

NARRATOR: Serpent ceaselessly circling.

EVE: Sees superior?

SERPENT: Yesss, superior.

NARRATOR: Serpent stops. Silence. Servant snatches sacred center seed and savors.

EVE: Sweet.

NARRATOR: So, servant savors and sees.

SERPENT: Yesss.

NARRATOR: Celestial sadness. Serpent smirks. *(Pause)* So sin. *(Pause)* So suffering.

Christ's Body

by Kevin Stoltz

Running Time: 5 minutes

Themes: The Body of Christ, spiritual gifts, community

Scripture Reference: 1 Corinthians 12:12-31

Synopsis: Readers theatre for four people, can be a mixture of male and female voices, about the Church being the Body of Christ.

Cast:
>   READER 1
>   READER 2
>   READER 3
>   READER 4

Production Notes: The readers start by forming a single line. Reader 1 faces the audience with the other readers directly behind Reader 1.

READER 1 *(softly):* Listen. Listen to the body.

READERS 2, 3, 4 *(softly):* The body is alive.

READER 1 *(excited):* This body is alive!

READER 2, 3, 4 *(softly):* This body is alive!

READER 1: This body is alive!

READER 2 *(steps to SL and faces audience):* The body breathes.

READER 1: From the breath of God.

READER 3 *(steps to SR and faces audience):* The body moves.

READER 1: And does the will of God.

READER 4 *(steps to SL, between READER 1 and READER 2, faces the audience):* The body sees and hears, touches and smells.

READER 1: And tastes the pain of our broken world.

ALL: The body is you—the Church.

READER 1, 3: Some are hands.

"Christ's Body" is taken from *The Lamb and the Wolf*. Copyright © 1998 by Kevin Stoltz. All print rights administered by Lillenas® Publishing Co. All rights reserved. Printed in the United States.

READERS 2, 4: Some are feet.

READERS 2, 4: Some are arms.

READERS 2, 3: Some are legs.

READER 4: Another is an ear.

READER 1: One could be the mouth.

READER 3: Others are the eyes.

READER 2: While some are fingers.

READERS 1, 3: Some are toes.

READERS 2, 4: We are still . . .

READERS 1, 3: one body.

ALL: One body!

READER 4: We are varied.

READER 3: We are different.

READER 2: Uniquely set apart.

READER 1: But the same Spirit

READER 4: controls us

READER 3: for a single

READER 2: purpose . . .

READER 1: To do the work of God.

READER 2: Many members.

READER 3: Many needs.

READER 4: Many functions.

ALL: For a healthy body, whole and complete.

(Immediately each READER turns his/her back to the audience. When each READER starts the next few lines, he/she turns toward the audience and mimes as if talking on the phone. Each READER begins in while the previous READER is talking. The sound should be chaotic.)

READER 3: Hello, Pastor? I just called to let you know that I won't be able to help lead the singing (READER 4*) next Sunday . . .

READER 4: Hello, I just wanted to let you know that I decided not to teach the children's Sunday School class this (READER 1) next quarter. I'm sure you can find someone else! (READER 2*)

READER 1: No, I'm afraid I don't have enough time to sing in the choir this year. (READER 3)

READER 2: Donate blood? Are you crazy? I mean, I would if I could, but I just can't today. (READER 4)

*READER 3: Let someone else do the sound and lighting for the play. I've got better things to do.

*READER 4: No, I don't have time to answer the teenage crisis hot lines. Someone else can listen.

(End of phone conversations; next part is fast-paced.)

READER 1: Someone else can work at the shelter.

READER 2: Someone else can go to the nursing home.

READER 3: Someone else can visit the prisoners.

READER 4: Someone else can volunteer at the boys' club.

READER 2: Someone else can visit the hospice.

ALL: Someone else! *(Pause then slower)*

READER 1: But not I.

READER 4: Not I.

READER 2: Not I.

READER 3: Not I.

(Pause)

READERS 1, 2: The body.

READERS 3, 4: The body.

ALL: What was once whole

READERS 1, 3: has become

READERS 3, 4: fragmented,

READERS 4, 2: torn,

READER 1: crippled,

READER 3: and dying.

READER 4: This is my body, which is broken for you.

READER 2: This is my blood, which is spilled for you.

READER 3: The new covenant, a new life.

READER 1: The Lord had His body broken for us, to give us His gift of new life.

READERS 2, 4: The body.

READERS 1, 3: His body.

READERS 2, 4: A gift.

READERS 1, 3: Our gift.

ALL: Of life!

READER 1: Share His brokenness. Share His life!

READERS 2, 4: Be His hands.

READERS 1, 3: Hold the people with His love.

READERS 2, 4: Be His feet.

READERS 1, 3: Search for the lost ones that need His love.

READERS 2, 4: Remember His body, remember His blood.

ALL: In His image

READERS 1, 2, 3: the body

READERS 1, 2: becomes

READER 1: one. *(Pause)*

ALL: Amen.

(All the READERS *then exit the stage together.)*

Jesus Heals a Man Born Blind

by Bette Dale Moore

Running Time: Approximately 5 minutes

Theme: The healing power of Jesus

Scripture Reference: John 9

Synopsis: The story of Jesus healing the blind man is told in readers theatre style.

Cast:
    ONE—Male
    TWO—Male
    THREE—Male

TWO *(speaking to audience):* As Jesus went along, He saw a man blind from birth. His disciples asked Him,

THREE *(disciple):* Rabbi, who sinned, this man or his parents, that he was born blind?

ONE *(Jesus):* Neither this man nor his parents sinned. But this happened so that the work of God might be displayed in his life. As long as it is day, we must do the work of Him who sent me. Night is coming when no one can work. While I am in the world, I am the light of the world.

TWO: Having said this, He spit on the ground, made some mud with the saliva, and put it on the man's eyes.

ONE: Go . . . wash in the pool of Siloam.

TWO: So the man went and washed, and came home seeing. His neighbors and those who had formerly seen him begging asked,

THREE *(neighbor, skeptical):* Isn't this the same man who used to sit and beg?

TWO: Some claimed that he was. Other said,

ONE *(another neighbor):* No, he only looks like him.

TWO: But he himself insisted,

THREE *(blind man):* I am the man!

Copyright © 1997 by Bette Dale Moore. All print rights administered by Lillenas® Publishing Co. All rights reserved. Printed in the United States.

One *(aggressively skeptical):* How then were your eyes opened?

Three: The man they call Jesus made some mud and put it on my eyes. He told me to go to Siloam and wash. So I went and washed, and then I could see.

One: Where is this man?

Three: I don't know.

Two: They brought to the Pharisees the man who had been blind. Now the day on which Jesus had made the mud and opened the man's eyes was a Sabbath. Therefore, the Pharisees also asked him how he had received his sight.

Three *(patiently repeats):* He put mud on my eyes, and I washed and now I see.

Two: Some of the Pharisees said,

One *(pompous Pharisee):* This man is not from God, for He does not keep the Sabbath.

Two: But others said,

Three *(sincere Pharisee):* How can a sinner do such miraculous signs?

Two: So they were divided. Finally, they turned again to the blind man.

One *(still pompous):* What have you to say about Him? It was your eyes He opened.

Three *(blind man, overwhelmed with emotion):* He is a prophet.

Two: The Jews still did not believe that he had been blind and had received his sight until they sent for the man's parents.

One *(demanding):* Is this your son?

Three *(skeptical Pharisee):* Is this the one you say was born blind?

One: How is it that now he can see?

Two *(Jewish mother):* We know he is our son, and we know he was born blind. But how he can see now, or who opened his eyes, we don't know. Ask him. He is of age; he will speak for himself.

One: His parents said this because they were afraid of the Jews, for already the Jews had decided that anyone who acknowledged that Jesus was the Christ would be put out of the synagogue. That was why his parents said,

Two: He is of age; ask him.

Three: A second time they summoned the man who had been blind.

One *(Pharisee, pompous):* Give glory to God. We know this man is a sinner.

Two: He replied,

THREE *(blind man):* Whether He is a sinner or not, I don't know. One thing I do know. I was blind but now I see!

ONE *(harshly):* What did He do to you? How did He open your eyes?

THREE *(irritated, somewhat sarcastic):* I have told you already and you did not listen. Why do you want to hear it again? Do you want to become His disciples too?

TWO: Then they hurled insults at him and said,

ONE *(enraged):* You are this fellow's disciple.

TWO *(Pharisee, angry):* We are disciples of Moses!

ONE: We know that God spoke to Moses

TWO: . . . but as for this fellow

ONE/TWO *(together):* . . . we don't even know where He comes from!

(TWO *drops character.*)

THREE *(feigning astonishment):* Now that is remarkable. You don't know where He comes from, yet He opened my eyes. We know that God does not listen to sinners. He listens to the godly man who does His will. Nobody has ever heard of opening the eyes of a man born blind. If this man were not from God, He could do nothing.

TWO: To this they replied,

ONE: You were steeped in sin at birth; how dare you lecture us!

TWO: And they threw him out. Jesus heard that they had thrown him out, and when He found him, He said,

ONE *(Jesus, gently):* Do you believe in the Son of Man?

THREE *(discouraged):* Who is He, sir? Tell me so that I may believe in Him.

ONE: You have now seen Him; in fact, He is the one speaking with you.

TWO: Then the man said,

THREE *(with great emotion):* Lord, I believe!

TWO: And he worshiped Him.

ONE *(Jesus):* For judgment I have come into this world, so that the blind will see and those who see will turn out to be blind.

TWO: Some Pharisees who were with Him heard Him say this and asked,

THREE *(Pharisee, indignant):* What? Are we blind too?

TWO: And Jesus said,

ONE: If you were blind, you would not be guilty of sin; but now that you claim you can see, your guilt remains.

(Slight pause)

ALL: May God bless the reading of His holy Word.

The End

Condemned

by Dave Tippett

Running Time: Approximately 5 minutes

Themes: Maundy Thursday, Good Friday, Easter

Scripture Reference: Matthew 27:11-26

Synopsis: Jesus is condemned to death.

Cast: Adults of either gender
>   Reader 1
>   Reader 2
>   Reader 3
>   Reader 4

Production Note: Room is dark. Each Reader is holding a candle and reads by its light. Background music needs to be dark and foreboding.

(Readers *take their places, one in each corner of the room, in the dark as music fades in.*)

Reader 1: Jesus was placed before the governor who questioned Him: "Are you the 'King of the Jews'"?

Reader 2: Jesus said, "If you say so."

Reader 3: But when the accusations rained down hot and heavy from the high priests and religious leaders, Jesus said—

Reader 4: nothing. *(Pause)* Pilate asked Him,

Reader 1: "Do you hear that long list of accusations? Aren't you going to say something?"

Reader 2: Jesus kept silent—not a word from His mouth. The governor was impressed.

Reader 4: Really impressed.

Reader 3: It was an old custom during the Feast for the governor to pardon a single prisoner named by the crowd.

Reader 4: At the time, they had the infamous Barabbas in prison.

Reader 3: With the crowd before him, Pilate said,

Copyright © 2005 by Dave Tippett. All print rights administered by Lillenas® Publishing Co. All rights reserved. Printed in the United States.

READER 1: "Which prisoner do you want me to pardon: Barabbas, or Jesus the so-called Christ?"

READER 2: He knew it was through sheer spite that they had turned Jesus over to him.

READER 3: While court was still in session, Pilate's wife sent him a message:

READER 4: "Don't get mixed up in judging this noble man. I've just been through a long and troubled night because of a dream about him."

READER 1: A long and troubled night.

READER 2: A long and troubled night.

READER 3: A long *(pause)* and troubled night.

READER 1: About Him.

READER 4: Meanwhile, the high priests and religious leaders had talked the crowd into asking for the pardon of Barabbas and the execution of Jesus. The governor asked,

READER 1: "Which of the two do you want me to pardon?"

ALL *(staggered, echo):* "Barabbas!"

READER 1: "Then what do I do with Jesus, the so-called Christ?"

ALL *(staggered, echo):* "Nail Him to a cross!"

READER 1: He objected, "But for what crime?"

READER 2: What crime?

READER 3: What crime?

READER 4: What crime?

READER 1: But the crowd yelled all the louder,

ALL: "Nail Him to a cross!"

(Pause)

READER 3: When Pilate saw that he was getting nowhere and that a riot was imminent,

READER 4 . . . he took a basin of water and washed his hands in full sight of the crowd, saying,

READER 1: "I'm washing my hands of responsibility for this man's death."

READER 2: Washing my hands.

READER 3: Washing my hands.

READER 4: Washing our hands.

READER 1: From now on, it's in your hands. You're judge and jury.

ALL *(staggered echo):* Judge and jury. All of us. Wet hands.

(Pause)

READER 2: The crowd answered,

ALL: "We'll take the blame, we and our children after us."

READER 2 *(almost a whisper):* Take the blame.

(Music comes up; lights up on a whipping post/bench; angry men's voices can be heard.)

READER 1: Then Pilate pardoned Barabbas. And Pilate then took Jesus and had Him whipped.

(Let music and crowd noise build along with sound of whipping.)

READER 2: The soldiers—

READER 3: having braided a crown from thorns—

READER 4: set it on His head—

READER 1: threw a purple robe over Him—

READER 2: and approached Him with,

ALL: "Hail, King of the Jews!"

READER 1: Then they greeted Him with—

READER 2: slaps in the face.

READER 3: And much worse.

(Long pause, music builds to climax, then quick silence.)

READER 4 *(quietly):* It begins.

READER 1: Taking the blame. *(Blows out candle)*

READER 2: For us and our— *(Blows out candle)*

READER 3: children after us. *(Blows out candle)*

READER 4: A long and troubled night . . . *(pause)* begins. *(Blows out candle)*

(In total darkness, after long pause.)

READER 2 *(very quiet):* What crime?

Love's Gift

by Coley Fisher

Running Time: 6-8 minutes

Themes: Christmas and the true meaning of Christmas, children's Christmas readers theatre, giving

Scripture References: Luke 2:1-20; John 3:16

Synopsis: At Christmas time children are often bombarded by the media's message that expensive gifts are always the best. Unfortunately, this is so far from the authentic meaning of Christmas. For when all is said and done, the best gift to unwrap at Christmastime and all year long is "Love's Gift" . . . the gift of a loving Savior sent by a heavenly Father to a very needy world.

Cast: 3 girls and 3 boys
  VOICE 1
  VOICE 2
  VOICE 3
  VOICE 4
  VOICE 5
  VOICE 6

Production Notes: This readers theatre was written for a group of 5-8 year-olds to present at their school's Christmas chapel program. The children perform using scripts. You can choreograph your own hand motions for the children to do where appropriate, which can be a hybrid of American Sign Language and phrase-related choreographed gestures. The gestures are performed by all the speakers, regardless of which "voice" is delivering dialogue. Though written for 6 voices originally, it is easily adapted for additional voices—male or female. To keep the proper pacing, rehearse the children with a rhythmic structure to help the flow of dialogue and unison parts. For added effect, use kid-created crayon drawings to punctuate the story via PowerPoint or slide show. Include drawing of wrapped gifts, a family around a Christmas tree, boys and girls, star-filled night skies, one large star, an angel, a chorus of angels, the stable exterior, baby Jesus in the manger, shepherds, wise men with gifts, and a closing slide of a gift with the text from John 3:16 over the image.

ALL: It's Christmas time, when kids are mostly thinking about presents and toys.

Copyright © 2004 by Coley Fisher. All print rights administered by Lillenas® Publishing Co. All rights reserved. Printed in the United States.

ALL GIRLS: Lots of gifts for the girls . . .

ALL BOYS: Lots of gifts for the boys.

VOICE 1: But we need to remember the real reason for giving.

VOICE 2: The reason that brings so many blessings to living.

ALL: Well . . .

VOICE 3: There was a time in our world long, long ago.

VOICE 4: When people lived without knowing—

ALL: How God loved them so.

VOICE 5: He tried to send teachers and prophets to show them how to obey.

VOICES 1, 3: But they chose not to listen to what God had to say.

(Beat)

VOICE 6: To get the world's attention something had to be done.

VOICE 2: God promised a love gift.

(Beat)

VOICES 1, 3: A gift for everyone.

VOICE 4: Forgiveness was needed for all the people's wrong choices.

VOICES 2, 5: The world cried for . . .

ALL: Mercy!

VOICE 6: And God heard their voices.

(Beat)

VOICE 1: It was

ALL: hundreds

VOICE 1: of years 'till the promise came true.

VOICES 4, 6: Then God sent the love gift . . .

VOICE 3: Like He promised to do!

(Beat)

VOICE 2: He chose Mary and Joseph to help with His plan.

VOICES 5, 6: He chose to send love

ALL: to make the world understand.

(Beat)

VOICE 4: To obey the King's law, they traveled to Bethlehem town.

VOICES 1, 3: But there was no room at the inn.

ALL: Not a room could be found.

VOICE 2: So, instead of a warm room, in a stable they stayed.

VOICE 5: With no bed for comfort.

ALL: Just some fresh hay.

VOICE 4: The night that it happened was ordinary.

(Beat)

VOICE 1: Just plain

VOICES 6, 2: Then some shepherds saw something . . .

VOICE 3: they couldn't explain.

VOICES 5, 1: You see, the sheep were asleep as the shepherds stood by . . .

VOICE 4: the stars began to sparkle . . .

ALL: and lit up the night sky.

VOICE 1: The shepherds looked up to see angels everywhere.

VOICES 2, 4: It was such a strange sight, so the shepherds were scared.

(Beat)

VOICE 5: The angels were singing praises in a beautiful chorus.

VOICE 3: They were sent to tell the world . . .

ALL: what God had done for us.

VOICE 4: There's going to be a gift sent to you *(beat)* that won't need unwrapping.

VOICE 2: So, listen to us and you'll know what's happening.

VOICE 1: The love gift will bring life, *(beat)* hope, *(beat)* and joy.

VOICE 6: It's a very special package—

ALL: A Baby boy!

VOICE 3, 5: This present won't be like anything the world has ever known.

VOICE 2: No money bought this gift—

VOICE 4: Just love alone!

VOICE 1: So if you want to find this gift,

ALL: . . . and if you really do care . . .

VOICE 3: you have to travel far so you can get there.

(Beat)

VOICE 5: Follow the big star.

VOICES 4, 6: It will mark the spot.

VOICE 2: You'll be glad you did.

ALL: Maybe more than you thought.

VOICE 1: You won't find a palace or a throne for a king . . .

(Beat)

VOICES 3, 6: just a humble stable holding a marvelous thing!

(Beat)

VOICE 2: So, the shepherds were faithful and followed the star.

VOICE 5: And there were wise men who came.

(Beat)

ALL: They traveled from far.

VOICES 1, 4: All the people rejoiced.

VOICE 3: When they saw the Child.

VOICE 6: And the Baby and parents rested for a while.

ALL: True to the words the angels had said,

VOICE 5: They found the Christ child in a manger bed.

(Beat)

VOICE 2: At once, the shepherds rejoiced and dropped to their knees.

(Beat)

VOICE 1: And all who came worshiped,

ALL: . . . like the scriptures decreed.

VOICE 4: Yes, all who gathered worshiped the tiny king.

VOICES 3, 6: For they knew the forgiveness this love gift would bring.

VOICE 5: This was the love gift that would set the world free.

VOICE 2: Because the Father sent His Son . . .

ALL: For you and for me.

VOICE 1: A love gift was sent.

VOICE 4: A purchase was made.

VOICES 5, 6: God's Son was the purchase and forgiveness the trade.

ALL: So you see . . .

VOICE 3: God's love can give gifts that money can't buy.

VOICES 1, 2: No matter how much *(beat)* a person could try.

ALL: It's Christmas time,

VOICE 4: And there will be many presents to enjoy . . .

ALL: But, remember love's gift. *(Beat)* A tiny Baby boy.

(Beat)

ALL: Merry Christmas!

(On a screen, project the Bible verse John 3:16.)

Notes

Notes

Notes

Notes

Notes